Susannah Reed

Super Minds

Teacher's Resource Book 1

CAMBRIDGE
UNIVERSITY PRESS

CAMBRIDGE
UNIVERSITY PRESS

University Printing House, Cambridge CB2 8BS, United Kingdom

One Liberty Plaza, 20th Floor, New York, NY 10006, USA

477 Williamstown Road, Port Melbourne, VIC 3207, Australia

314–321, 3rd Floor, Plot 3, Splendor Forum, Jasola District Centre, New Delhi – 110025, India

79 Anson Road, #06–04/06, Singapore 079906

Cambridge University Press is part of the University of Cambridge.

It furthers the University's mission by disseminating knowledge in the pursuit of education, learning and research at the highest international levels of excellence.

www.cambridge.org
Information on this title: www.cambridge.org/9781107666047

© Cambridge University Press 2012

First published 2012
Reprinted 2019

Printed in Great Britain by CPI Group (UK) Ltd, Croydon CR0 4YY

A catalogue record for this publication is available from the British Library

ISBN 978-1-107-66604-7 Teacher's Resource Book 1
ISBN 978-0-521-14855-9 Student's Book with DVD-ROM 1
ISBN 978-0-521-14857-3 Workbook 1
ISBN 978-0-521-22061-3 Teacher's Book 1
ISBN 978-0-521-22136-8 Class Audio CDs 1
ISBN 978-0-521-22026-2 Flashcards 1
ISBN 978-0-521-94858-0 Classware and Interactive DVD-ROM 1

Contents

Introduction

The Teacher's Resource Book contains photocopiable worksheets which provide extra language practice for those teachers and students following *Super Minds* Level 1. In addition, each of the ten Student's Book units is provided with two progress tests, one based on listening and one on reading, covering the same content as the photocopiable worksheets.

What do the photocopiable worksheets provide?

The photocopiable worksheets have been carefully designed to reinforce and provide extra practice of the work done in class. They focus on the language introduced in each unit of Level 1 of the course and do not introduce or use any additional or unfamiliar language.

Each worksheet has accompanying teacher's notes with suggestions for exploitation in the classroom, together with suggested Optional follow-up activities.

There are four worksheets for each main unit in Level 1:

Worksheet 1: This worksheet focuses on the key vocabulary presented on the opening page of each unit in the Student's Book. The vocabulary area is identified at the foot of the worksheet and items are listed in detail in the teacher's notes.

Worksheet 2: This worksheet focuses on the language presented and practised in the first grammar lesson of each unit (on the second page of each unit in the Student's Book). The target language is detailed in the teacher's notes.

Worksheet 3: This worksheet focuses on the language presented and practised in the second grammar lesson of each unit (on the fourth page of each unit in the Student's Book). Once again, the target language is detailed in the teacher's notes.

Worksheet 4: This worksheet is based on the CLIL content of each unit (covered on pages seven and eight in each unit of the Student's Book).

In addition, there are three worksheets provided for use with the Friends unit.

How can the worksheets be used?

The worksheets can be used in a number of ways:

- **The first three worksheets in each unit** have been designed so that students can work on them either individually or as part of pair or class activities. For individual work, the worksheets could be used by those students who finish class activities more quickly than others. Alternatively, they can be set for homework. For pair or class activities, the worksheets can be used when additional practice is necessary, for revision or as an alternative activity when there is a gap or change in your usual lesson routine. Suggestions on how to use the worksheets in different ways are included in the accompanying teacher's notes.

- **The fourth worksheet in each unit** (the CLIL worksheet) is intended to be used communicatively, for pair, small group or class activities. These worksheets include games and craft activities. Suggestions on how to use these worksheets are also included in the accompanying teacher's notes.

What activity types do the worksheets provide?

The worksheets provide a range of games and puzzles and, at this level, activities which require the students to read and write words and phrases.

All activities (apart from the tests) are designed to be used without an audio accompaniment.

The teacher's notes and Optional follow-up activities contain references to some well-known traditional games and activities. These include:

Simon says! Call out instructions for students to follow. If you say an instruction with *Simon says* at the beginning of it, e.g. *Simon says, stand up*, they should do as you say. Without the instruction *Simon says* at the beginning, e.g. *Stand up*, students should do nothing. If they follow an instruction wrongly, they are 'out' and have to sit down. They can also play this game in small groups.

Matching pairs Students play this game in pairs or small groups. They lay out sets of cards face down on a table, then take turns to turn up two cards at a time, one from each set, and name them. If the two cards match, they keep them. If they don't, they replace the cards in their original places on the table. As the game continues, students begin to remember where the cards are and start matching pairs from memory. The winner is the student who has the most matching pairs at the end of the game.

Bingo Students choose three or four words or pictures from a vocabulary group or groups, e.g. clothes and colours. Call out words, or descriptions of the pictures, e.g. *a blue skirt*. When students hear you call out something that they have chosen, they cross it out. The first one to cross out all the words or pictures they have chosen calls out *Bingo!*

Spinners As an alternative to using dice in board games, students can make and use a spinner (see page 14). The spinner is made by drawing a circle and then dividing it into six equal segments by drawing lines. Students should then cut off the 'arc' of each segment on the outside of the circle so that there is a straight edge going across the widest part of each segment. They then write the numbers from one to six, one in each segment. Finally, a hole is made in the centre of the circle and a pencil pushed through. Students can then spin the pencil with their thumb and first two fingers. The number it rests on each time is used to play the game.

Using the end-of-unit progress tests

There are two progress tests for each of the ten units in the Level 1 Student's Book.

Introductory notes for the progress tests, teacher's notes, tapescripts and keys can be found at the back of the book from page 75 onwards.

Worksheet 1: I'm Whisper.

Using the worksheet

- This matching activity establishes the main characters in the book.

- Students match the silhouettes with the pictures of the characters and the correct speech bubbles. The first one has been done for them as an example. They then draw in any details and colour the silhouettes.

- Students can then work in pairs to ask and answer about the characters on the worksheet. Student A points to one character and asks *What's your name?* Student B answers, using the first person, e.g. *I'm Whisper.*

KEY: **2d** I'm Thunder. **3a** I'm Misty. **4b** I'm Flash.

Optional follow-up activity: Play a name game. Allocate each student in the class the name of a main character to remember (*Whisper*, *Thunder*, *Flash* or *Misty*). Call out one of the names, e.g. *Whisper*. All the students allocated this name stand up. Ask individual students *What's your name?* They reply with *I'm (Whisper)*.

Worksheet 2: I'm three.

Using the worksheet

- This counting and matching activity revises numbers and practises *How old are you? I'm … .*

- Students read the speech bubbles for the children on the worksheet and match them to the correct cake by counting the candles. Students can then check their work in pairs. For each child on the worksheet, Student A points and asks *How old are you?* Student B replies with the correct age, e.g. *I'm three.* They then swap roles.

- Students then draw their own candles on the cake at the bottom of the worksheet and complete the sentence with the number for their own age.

KEY: Activity 1: **2c**, **3b**, **4f**, **5e**, **6a**; Activity 2: answers will vary.

Optional follow-up activity: Practise numbers by playing a number clapping game in class. Clap a number of times, e.g. three. Students listen and clap the same number of times, then say the number. Make this harder or easier by varying the speed and rhythm of your clapping. You can also call out numbers for students to make their own clapping patterns to.

Worksheet 3: Colours

Using the worksheet

- This Bingo activity practises the colours *red*, *yellow*, *blue*, *green*, *purple*, *orange*. It also revises numbers 1 to 6.

- Students revise colours by reading the words and colouring in the circles in those colours. Then, on the Bingo card, they colour each balloon in a different colour of their choice in any order.

- Play Bingo (see page 4). Make sentences using numbers and colours, e.g. *Number 1 is red*. Students who have coloured the first balloon red put a tick in the box next to it. Repeat this procedure using different numbers and colours until one student has ticked all their balloons. They call out *Bingo!*

Optional follow-up activity: Students cut out the pictures in the Bingo card and use them to make a set of colour cards. They then use these to play a matching game in class. Students take turns to choose one of their cards and say, e.g. *a purple balloon*. Other students hold up their cards with a purple balloon on them. Or students can make sentences combining numbers and colours, e.g. *Number 3 is purple*. This time, only students who have coloured balloon number 3 in purple can hold it up.

Worksheet 1: I'm Whisper.

Match and draw lines.

I'm Misty.

I'm Whisper.

I'm Flash.

I'm Thunder.

Vocabulary: I'm Whisper, Misty, Flash, Thunder

© Cambridge University Press 2012   *Super Minds* Teacher's Resource Book Level 1   7

Worksheet 2: I'm three.

1 Read, count and match.

1 I'm three.
2 I'm eight.
3 I'm six.
4 I'm nine.
5 I'm seven.
6 I'm ten.

a
b
c
d
e
f

2 How old are you? Draw and write.

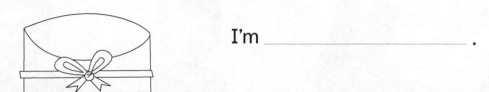

I'm _____ .

Numbers: 1 to 10

Super Minds Teacher's Resource Book Level 1   © Cambridge University Press 2012   **PHOTOCOPIABLE**

Worksheet 3: Colours

1 **Colour the circles.**

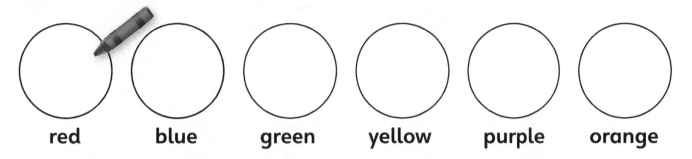

red   blue   green   yellow   purple   orange

2 **Choose colours and colour the balloons.**
Then play Bingo.

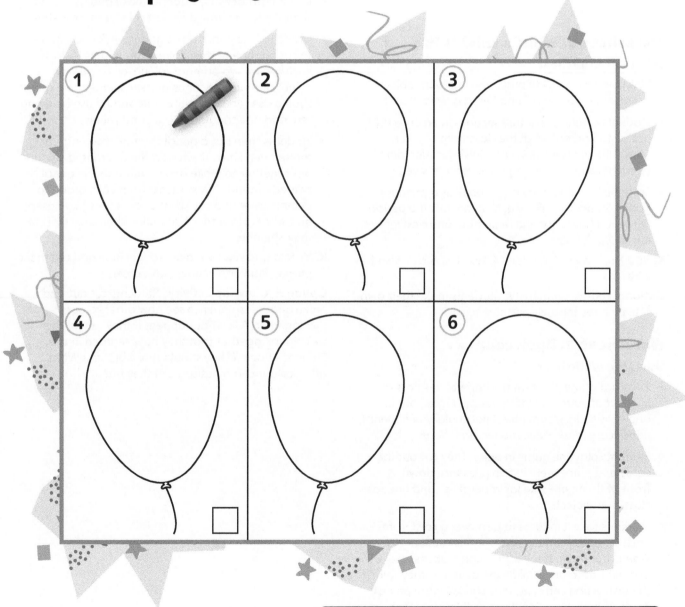

Colours: red, blue, green, orange, purple, yellow

© Cambridge University Press 2012   *Super Minds* Teacher's Resource Book Level 1

1 At school

Worksheet 1: Classroom objects

Using the worksheet

- This drawing and matching activity practises the vocabulary for classroom objects *bag, book, rubber, desk, pen, pencil, ruler, pencil case, notebook*.

- Students complete the drawings by tracing round the outlines. They then match the pictures to the correct words.

KEY: **2** book, **3** rubber, **4** desk, **5** pen, **6** pencil, **7** ruler, **8** notebook, **9** pencil case

Optional follow-up activity: Students use the worksheet for a colour dictation in pairs. They take turns to choose a colour for each object, dictate it to their partner and both, secretly, colour it in appropriately, e.g. *a red pencil case*, or *pencil case – red*. At the end they compare their worksheets to make sure they match.

Worksheet 2: What's this? Is it a … ?

Using the worksheet

- This colouring activity practises classroom objects, *What's this? Is it a … ?* and *Yes, it is. / No, it isn't.*

- Students colour the dotted sections in each picture puzzle to find out what the classroom object is. They then answer the *What's this?* question next to each picture by circling the correct answer.

- Students can then play this in pairs as a memory game. Student A asks, e.g. *Number 1. Is it a pencil?* Student B has to try and remember and answer *Yes, it is* or *No, it isn't.*

KEY: **2** No, it isn't. **3** Yes, it is. **4** Yes, it is. **5** No, it isn't. **6** Yes, it is.

Optional follow-up activity: Students make their own puzzle pictures for their partners to solve.

Worksheet 3: Open your …

Using the worksheet

- This card game practises the imperatives *Pass me a … , Sit at your … , Open your … , Close your …* and revises classroom object vocabulary *pen, pencil, pencil case, desk, ruler, rubber, bag, book.*

- Students play the game in pairs. They cut out the cards and place them in two piles face down in front of them: one pile for imperatives and one for classroom objects.

- Students take it in turns to turn over a card from each pile and read the resulting instruction, e.g. *Open your book.* If the instruction makes sense, their partner has to do or mime the action. If they follow the instruction correctly, they can keep the pair of cards. If the instruction is impossible, e.g. *Open your rubber*, students replace the cards somewhere into

each pile. The winner of the game is the student who has the most cards when all possible pairs have been matched up.

Optional follow-up activity: Students write their own sentences with similar instructions for a class message game. These can be either the instructions in the worksheet or other imperatives they remember. Students write their messages on a slip of paper and put them into a bag or box. Play the game by asking volunteers to come to the front of the class, take a message from the box and act it out for the class to guess what the message is. The first student to guess correctly has the next turn.

Worksheet 4: Colours

Using the worksheet

- In this craft activity, students make and use colour spinners to see how different colours mix together.

- Divide the class into three groups. Ask each student to cut out one of their spinner templates. Assign each group two primary colours with which to colour alternate sections of their spinner: one group should use red and yellow, one should use blue and red, and one should use blue and yellow.

- Students then put a pencil through the centre of the spinner. Show them how the alternated colours mix together to make a new colour as the pencil is twirled around. Ask students from each group to demonstrate and say what colours they have used and what colour they can make when they twirl their spinners.

KEY: Red and yellow make orange. Blue and red make purple. Blue and yellow make green.

Optional follow-up activity: Students cut out and make another spinner to see how other colours mix together. Ask what happens if they use all the six colours together that they have learned in the Student's Book. (They should make brown.) What other colour combinations can they try?

1 Worksheet 1: Classroom objects

Complete the pictures. Then match the pictures and the words.

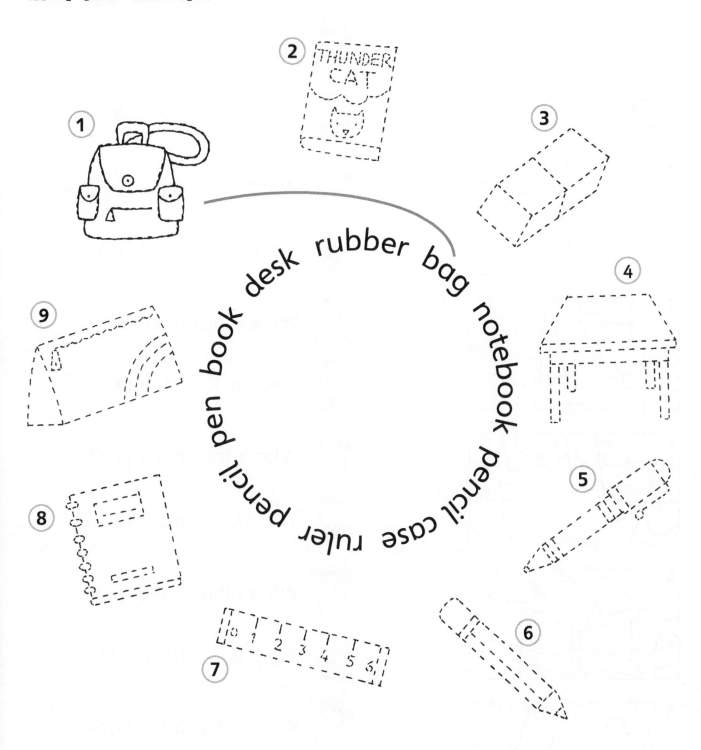

Vocabulary: Classroom objects

Worksheet 2: What's this? Is it a ... ?

Colour. Then circle the answer.

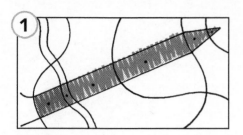
 What's this? Is it a ruler?
 Yes, it is.  No, it isn't.

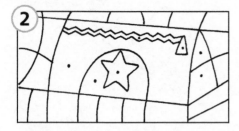
 What's this? Is it a notebook?
 Yes, it is.   No, it isn't.

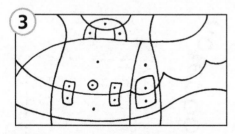
 What's this? Is it a bag?
 Yes, it is.   No, it isn't.

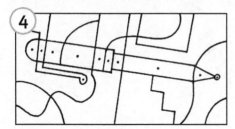
 What's this? Is it a pen?
 Yes, it is.   No, it isn't.

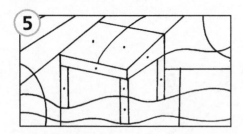
 What's this? Is it a rubber?
 Yes, it is.   No, it isn't.

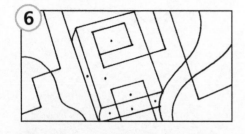
 What's this? Is it a book?
 Yes, it is.   No, it isn't.

Grammar 1: Questions and short answers

Super Minds Teacher's Resource Book Level 1   © Cambridge University Press 2012   **PHOTOCOPIABLE**

Cut out the cards and play.

Pass me a	desk	Open your	rubber
Sit at your	book	Close your	ruler
Close your	pencil	Pass me a	pencil case
Pass me a	pen	Open your	bag

Grammar 2: Imperatives

© Cambridge University Press 2012 *Super Minds* Teacher's Resource Book Level 1

Worksheet 4: Colours

Make a colour spinner.

  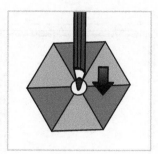 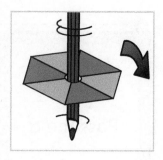

Cut out.   Colour.   Push.   Spin.

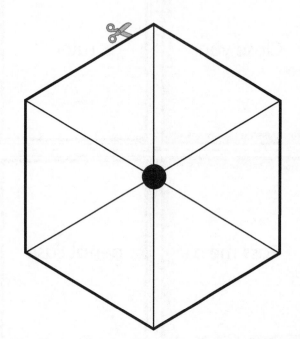 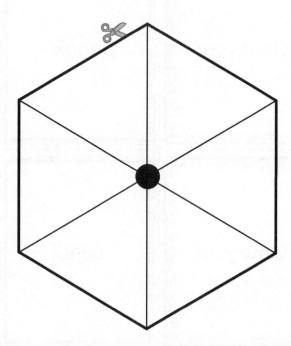

What colours can you make?

Art: Colours

Super Minds Teacher's Resource Book Level 1   © Cambridge University Press 2012   **PHOTOCOPIABLE**

② Let's play!

Worksheet 1: Toys

Using the worksheet

- This read and match activity practises recognising toy vocabulary *bike, go-kart, computer game, doll, car, kite, monster, ball, plane, train* and writing numbers 1 to 10.

- Students look at the toys and their numbers on the prize stall. They write the correct numbers on the relevant labels.

KEY: 2 doll, **3** computer game, **4** ball, **5** bike, **6** go-kart, **7** car, **8** train, **9** monster, **10** kite

Optional follow-up activity: Students play a simple prize game in pairs or small groups. They make number cards for numbers 1 to 10 and put them face down in front of them. Students then take turns to choose a number card and read it out, e.g. *4!* Their partner looks at the stall in the worksheet and tells them what they have won: *It's a ball!* Encourage students to say *Thank you.* This can also be played in class with small toys or classroom objects.

Worksheet 2: How old is he?

Using the worksheet

- Matching activity **1** practises recognising toy vocabulary. Reading activity **2** practises *his, her, he, she* and questions *What's his / her name? What's his / her favourite toy? How old is he / she?*

- Students read the description of each child and find and number the correct child in the picture.

- Students then complete the questions at the bottom of the worksheet by circling the correct word each time. They then ask the questions to their partner, who can answer either from memory or by checking back to the information in Activity 1.

KEY: Activity 1: **2**d, **3**c, **4**b; Activity 2: **1** she (five), **2** his (Ben), **3** her (her kite), **4** he (four)

Optional follow-up activity: Students make a class or group chart with their names, ages and pictures of their favourite toys and colours. They use this to play a guessing game in pairs. Student A describes another student from the chart, stating their age, favourite toy and colour, e.g. *She's eight. Her favourite colour is red. Her favourite toy is a bike.* Student B uses the information in the chart to guess who it is.

Worksheet 3: A long blue train

Using the worksheet

- This drawing activity practises ordering adjectives *long, old, small, ugly*; the colours *red, yellow, blue, green*; toys *monster, car, train, kite* and articles *a* and *an*.

- Starting at the top of the worksheet, students choose a stepping stone in each row to make a phrase using an adjective, colour and toy. They then draw and colour the toy in the toy box at the bottom to fit the phrase they have made. The first drawing has been done for them as an example. They can colour this in.

- Students then show and describe their pictures to the class.

- If appropriate, students can write the combinations they make, e.g. *an ugly red monster.*

KEY: Drawings will vary. Make sure that each phrase contains one word from each line of stepping stones, e.g. *a long blue train.* Students should also be careful to connect *a* with *long* or *small* and *an* with *old* or *ugly.*

Optional follow-up activity: Play a game of *Stepping Stones* in class. Write words onto pieces of paper or card. You could include other adjectives, colours and toys. Lay these on the floor in four rows as in the worksheet. Ask for a volunteer to stand at the start of the stepping stones. Call out a description, e.g. *an ugly red monster.* The volunteer has to step on the correct stepping stones as you call them out. Students can also take turns at calling out descriptions. This could also be played with small cards on a table. Students follow the stepping stones using their fingers.

Worksheet 4: What's next?

Using the worksheet

- This thinking activity revises vocabulary for toys *ball, doll, monster, car, plane*, shapes *triangle, circle, square*, classroom objects *pencil, book* and characters *Misty, Flash* and *Thunder.* It also introduces students to the mathematical principle of sequences.

- Students work out the sequences in each row. Help them with this concept as necessary. They then draw and label the missing item in each sequence.

- Students then make up their own sequence with one missing picture for a partner to solve. They can just draw the pictures or write words as well, as you prefer.

KEY: 2 monster, **3** book, **4** plane, **5** Misty

Optional follow-up activity: Play a sequence chain game round the class. Start the sequence off by giving three or four students the first words to say, e.g. *red, yellow, blue, red … .* Students continue the pattern of words round the class. Make the sequences easy or more difficult depending on the level of your class.

Read and write the numbers.

monster ☐

plane [1]

car ☐

ball ☐

go-kart ☐

doll ☐

train ☐

computer game ☐

kite ☐

bike ☐

Vocabulary: Toys

Worksheet 2: How old is he?

1 **Read and write the numbers.**

1
Her name's Kim. She's five.
Her favourite toy is her monster.

2
His name's Ben. He's eight.
His favourite toy is his ball.

3
Her name's Mia. She's seven.
Her favourite toy is her kite.

4
His name's Sam. He's four.
His favourite toy is his train.

2 **Choose and circle. Then ask a friend.**

1. How old is he / (she)?

2. What's his / her name?

3. What's his / her favourite toy?

4. How old is he / she?

Grammar 1: Present simple questions, 3rd person

© Cambridge University Press 2012 *Super Minds* Teacher's Resource Book Level 1 17

Worksheet 3: A long blue train

Choose, then draw lines. Draw your picture in the toy box.

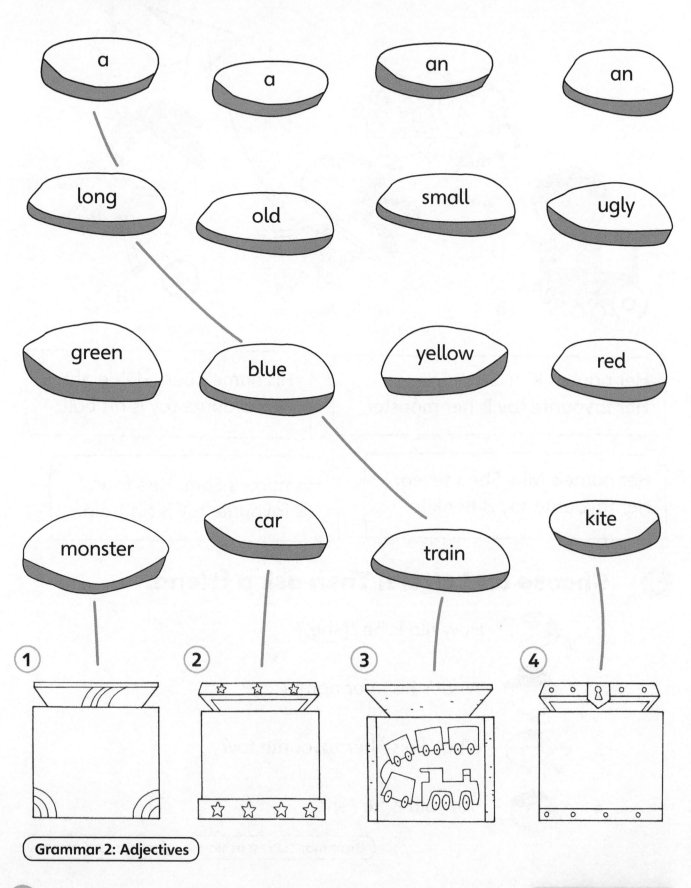

Super Minds Teacher's Resource Book Level 1   © Cambridge University Press 2012   **PHOTOCOPIABLE**

Grammar 2: Adjectives

Worksheet 4: What's next?

1 What's next? Draw and write.

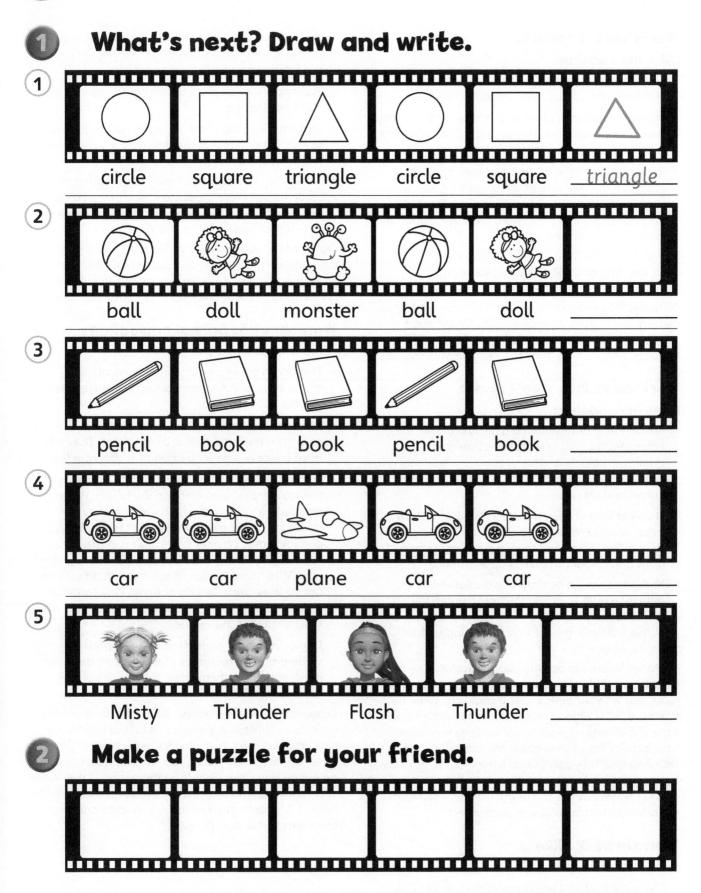

1 circle   square   triangle   circle   square   *triangle*

2 ball   doll   monster   ball   doll   _____

3 pencil   book   book   pencil   book   _____

4 car   car   plane   car   car   _____

5 Misty   Thunder   Flash   Thunder   _____

2 Make a puzzle for your friend.

_____ _____ _____ _____ _____ _____

Maths: Sequences

Worksheet 1: Animals

Using the worksheet

- This worksheet practises animal vocabulary *dog, elephant, cat, spider, frog, lizard, rat, duck*.

- Students match the silhouettes to the animals. They then label the pictures by copying the correct word each time from the word bank.

- Students then write the name of their favourite animal in the sentence at the bottom of the worksheet. They can choose an animal from the page, or teach them new words for their favourite animals if you prefer.

KEY: 2d (a dog); 3g (a lizard); 4a (a duck); 5b (an elephant); 6h (a cat); 7f (a frog); 8e (a spider)

Optional follow-up activity: Students play an animal mime game in pairs or small groups. One student mimes an animal from the worksheet for the others to guess. Alternatively, they can make animal sounds.

Worksheet 2: in / on / under

Using the worksheet

- This drawing and colouring activity practises the prepositions *in, on, under* and revises colours, classroom objects and toy vocabulary. Students will need coloured pencils in red, yellow, blue, green, purple and orange.

- Students look at the example in number **1**. Show them how to colour the spider in the appropriate colour. They then read the other sentences and draw and colour the spiders appropriately.

KEY: Spiders should be drawn and coloured as follows: a blue spider on the ball; a green spider in the bag; a yellow spider in the pencil case; a purple spider under the train; an orange spider on the book.

Optional follow-up activity: Do a class treasure hunt. Before class, hide about ten small objects around the room, e.g. on your desk, under a chair, etc. Write the names of these objects on the board for students to copy in a list onto a piece of paper. They then have to search for the objects round the classroom. When they find one, they don't say anything but write down its location on their piece of paper. The whole class checks answers at the end of the activity. Volunteers are asked to find and retrieve each object.

Worksheet 3: I like ...

Using the worksheet

- These reading and writing activities practise *I like* and *I don't like* and animal plurals.

- Students complete the chart with smilies according to the animals they like and don't like. They can do this either individually or in pairs, with one student saying what they like and don't like and the other recording their answers.

- Students then complete the sentences next to the chart accordingly.

- Students read the riddle in Flash's speech bubble to find out the animal she doesn't like (rats). They write this word into her speech bubble.

KEY: Activity 1: Answers will vary. Make sure that students complete the sentences with the plural version of the animal words and that the sentences match their smilies in the chart.

Optional follow-up activity: Students make up their own riddles of their likes and dislikes for their partners to read and guess. They can use animal vocabulary or revise another vocabulary set they know, e.g. toys.

Worksheet 4: Animal camouflage

Using the worksheet

- This board game practises animal vocabulary *snake, elephant, rat, frog, spider, crocodile, tiger, giraffe, butterfly, lizard*.

- Students play in pairs. They each choose an animal card from the bottom of the worksheet. They will need a dice or spinner (see page 4) and counters.

- Students take turns to throw the dice or spin the spinner and move around the board. When they land on a square with an animal they are collecting, they have to make a sentence about the animal, e.g. *It's a tiger. / The tiger is in the grass. / It's a big tiger.* and cross the animal name off their card. When they land on a square with an animal not on their card, they do nothing. Play continues round the board. The first student to cross out all their animals is the winner.

- Demonstrate the game first with a confident student and go round the class while students are playing, helping them make their sentences, as necessary.

Optional follow-up activity: Play a game of animal anagrams. Write some anagrams on the board, e.g. *ogd, leepthan, act, cudk, tar*. Students work in pairs to guess and write the words. Ask for volunteers to come and write the correct words on the board. If they write them correctly, the rest of the class have to act out the animal. Students can also make their own anagrams for others in the class to solve.

1 Match. Then write the words.

a rat   a duck   a cat   a spider   an elephant   a lizard   a dog   a frog

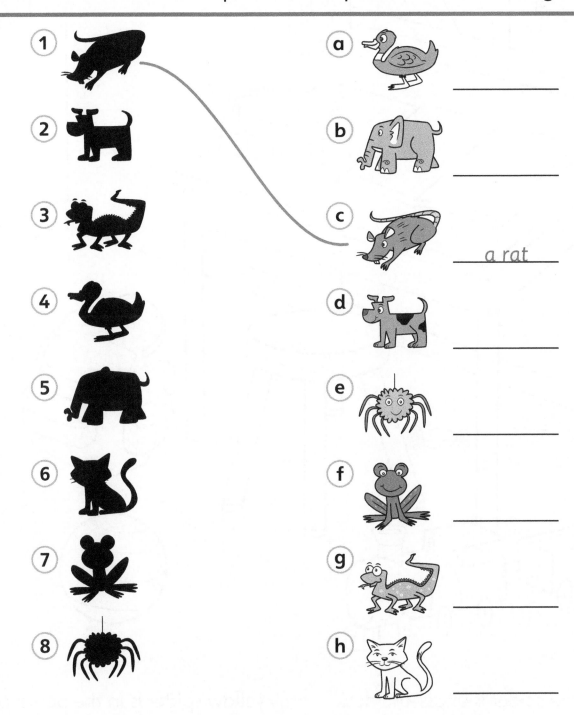

a rat

2 What's your favourite animal? Write.

My favourite animal is a / an _____ .

3 Worksheet 2: in / on / under

Read, draw and colour the spiders.

1 ~~A red spider is under the desk.~~

2 A blue spider is on the ball.

3 A green spider is in the bag.

4 A yellow spider is in the pencil case.

5 A purple spider is under the train.

6 An orange spider is on the book.

Grammar 1: Prepositions: *in, on, under*

Super Minds Teacher's Resource Book Level 1   © Cambridge University Press 2012   **PHOTOCOPIABLE**

Worksheet 3: I like ...

1 **Draw happy or sad faces. Then write.**

I like _____

_____

_____ .

I like _____

_____ , too.

I don't like _____

_____

_____ .

2 **Read and guess. Then write.**

I like ducks and cats. I like elephants and spiders. I like lizards and I like frogs, too. My favourite animals are dogs. I don't like

_____ .

Grammar 2: *like / don't like*, 1st person

© Cambridge University Press 2012 *Super Minds* Teacher's Resource Book Level 1

Worksheet 4: Animal camouflage

Play the camouflage game. Cross off the words.

A

snake elephant
frog spider rat

B

crocodile tiger giraffe
butterfly lizard

Science: Animal camouflage

4 Lunchtime

Worksheet 1: Food

Using the worksheet

- This crossword activity practises food vocabulary *cheese, cake, sandwich, carrot, sausage, peas, steak, banana, apple, pizza, chicken.*

- Students use the numbers under the pictures to complete the crossword, copying the words from the word bank.

KEY: 1 ↓ cake, **2** sandwich, **3** carrot, **4** sausage, **5** peas, **6** steak, **7** banana, **8** apple, **9** pizza, **10** chicken

Optional follow-up activity: Do a drawing dictation. Draw the foods on the board and check lexis. Then say some foods you like and don't like and your favourite food, e.g. *I like sandwiches and I like chicken. I like apples and bananas, too. My favourite food is pizza. I don't like steak.* Students listen and draw the things you say you like on a piece of paper. They don't draw any items you say you don't like. Students can also do this activity in pairs.

Worksheet 2: I've got ...

Using the worksheet

- These reading and writing activities practise *I've got / haven't got* and revise food vocabulary *cake, steak, pizza, peas, cheese, chicken, sandwich, carrots.*

- Students look at the picture of the boy with a cake and a sandwich. They complete the food poem by circling *I've got* or *I haven't got* in each sentence.

- Students then complete the second food poem by choosing and writing either *I've got* or *I haven't got* in each line. (There is no right or wrong answer.) They then read the poem aloud and draw all the items for which they've written *I've got* on the girl's plate.

KEY: Activity 1: **2** I haven't got, **3** I've got, **4** I've got; Activity 2: Answers will vary. Check that students have drawn the correct items on the plate according to how they've completed the poem.

Optional follow-up activity: Students write their own version of the food poem. They can either keep the rhyming words *cheese, peas, cake* and *steak* or they can write a version that doesn't rhyme.

Worksheet 3: Have we got any ... ?

Using the worksheet

- This reading and writing activity practises *Have we got any ... ? Yes, we have. / No, we haven't.* and food vocabulary *chicken, steak, banana, cheese, sandwich.*

- Students look at the pictures in the story and complete the speech bubbles with *Yes, we have.* or *No, we haven't.*, then fill in the missing food word in picture 5.

- In pairs, students can then act the story out.

KEY: **2** No, we haven't. **3** Yes, we have. **4** Yes, we have. **5** banana

Optional follow-up activity: Students make up their own version of the story, using different food combinations in their sandwiches. Write the nine lines of the dialogue on the board, leaving blanks for the food words and answers. Students copy this into their books and add their own food words to each line. Provide a list of food words for them to choose from if necessary. Students see who can invent the most delicious or most disgusting sandwich. They can then draw their sandwiches and display them, with their dialogues, in the classroom.

Worksheet 4: Growing tomatoes

Using the worksheet

- This reading activity explores the theme of growing fruit and vegetables. It revises adjectives, colours, imperatives and *have got.* You will need to introduce the new words *pot, water* and *seeds.*

- Ask students to look at the pictures first and explain that these show how to grow tomatoes. Students then look at the first picture and sentence c under it. This is the first instruction.

- Students read the instructions and write the correct letter next to each picture. They can colour the plants and the tomatoes in pictures 3 to 6 appropriately.

KEY: **2**a, **3**e, **4**f, **5**d, **6**b

Optional follow-up activity: Students use these instructions to try growing tomato plants in the classroom or at home. Other suitable vegetables include red peppers, peas and beans. Or you could try a variety of vegetables and see which are most successful.

Look and write the words.

> banana   chicken   ~~cheese~~   sandwich   sausage
> cake   steak   apple   pizza   peas   carrot

 1 → 1 ↓ 2 3 4 5

(crossword grid with 1 across spelled: c h e e s e)

 6   7   8   9   10

Vocabulary: Food

4 Worksheet 2: I've got ...

1 Look and circle *I've got* or *I haven't got* in the poem.

¹ I've got / I haven't got chicken,
² I've got / I haven't got steak,
³ I've got / I haven't got a sandwich,
⁴ I've got / I haven't got cake!

2 Write *I've got* or *I haven't got*. Then draw.

_____ carrots,
_____ peas,
_____ pizza,
_____ cheese!

Grammar 1: *have / haven't got*, 1st person

© Cambridge University Press 2012 *Super Minds* Teacher's Resource Book Level 1

Look. Write *Yes, we have.* or *No, we haven't.*
What sandwich has the boy got?

Grammar 2: Questions with *have got any*

Look at the pictures. Read and match.

 1 — C

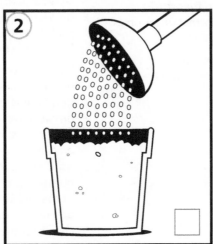 2 — ☐

 3 — ☐

 4 — ☐

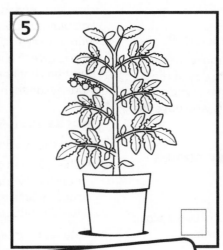 5 — ☐

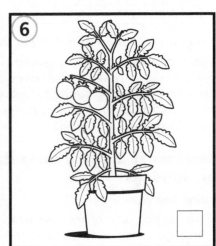 6 — ☐

a Water the seeds.

b Now the tomatoes are big. They are red.

c Put tomato seeds in a pot.

d Three small tomatoes are on the plant. They are green.

e You've got a small plant.

f Three yellow flowers are on the plant.

Science: Fruit and vegetables

5 Free time

Worksheet 1: Days of the week

Using the worksheet

- This worksheet practises the days of the week.

- Students circle the days of the week in the word search. They then write them in the correct order on the diary page.

- Students then find the characters' favourite day of the week in the word art puzzles and complete their speech bubbles.

KEY: Activity **1**

F						T	T
R	M	O	N	D	A	Y	H	U
I						U	E
D	S	U	N	D	A	Y	R	S
A						S	D
Y						D	A
W	E	D	N	E	S	D	A	Y
S	A	T	U	R	D	A	Y

Activity 2: Thunder, Friday; Whisper, Saturday

Optional follow-up activity: Students make their own word art puzzle based on their favourite day of the week for a partner to guess. Students can also do this as a class activity, finding other students who have the same favourite day as them.

Worksheet 2: I play computer games on Sundays.

Using the worksheet

- This writing activity and card game practises *I play, ride, go … -ing, on* and days of the week.

- Students label the activity pictures first, choosing an expression from the word bank each time.

- They then cut out the cards and combine them with a partner's to play a game in pairs. Students put their cards face down in two piles: one for activities and one for days of the week.

- Students take turns to turn over a card from each pile and use them to make a sentence, e.g. *I ride my pony on Saturdays.*

KEY: 2 ride my bike, **3** ride my pony, **4** go swimming, **5** play football, **6** play the piano

Optional follow-up activity: Students use the cards to play a game of *True or False* in pairs or small groups. Students turn over the cards and make sentences in the same way but this time their partners have to decide if the sentences are true for that student or not, e.g. *I go swimming on Mondays. False.* If the sentences are false they can also correct them, where appropriate, e.g. *I go swimming on Saturdays.*

Worksheet 3: Do you … ?

Using the worksheet

- This pyramid reading activity practises questions *Do you … at the weekend / on … ?* and short answers *Yes, I do / No, I don't.* Students follow a path to find out which character they are most like, based on what they do and don't do.

- Students work in pairs. Starting at the top of the activity, one student makes the question *Do you go swimming at the weekend?* If their partner answers *Yes, I do*, they follow the 'smiley' arrow to the question prompts for *Do you play football on Mondays?* However, if their partner answers *No, I don't*, they follow the 'other' arrow to the question prompts for *Do you play with your friends at the weekend?* They continue like this, moving down through the diagram until they come to the character their partner is most like.

Optional follow-up activity: Play a game of *Last man standing*. Students stand up. Ask a question, e.g. *Do you play computer games at the weekend?* Students who answer *Yes, I do* remain standing. Students who answer *No, I don't* sit down. Repeat with other questions until only one student is left standing. This student can then ask the questions.

Worksheet 4: My life

Using the worksheet

- This question and answer activity revises the question *What's your favourite … ?* and vocabulary for free time activities. It also encourages students to think about and compare their own lifestyles.

- Students write the answers to the questions for themselves first.

- They then work in groups of four. They ask the questions to the other three students in their group and record their answers. At the end of the activity, they check the answers and see who in the group shares the most favourites with them. They can feed this back to the class.

Optional follow-up activity: Use the findings of the questionnaires to record the whole class' favourites in a bar chart or poster. Remind students of the importance of having a healthy balance of work, rest and play in their lifestyles and praise them for the variety of activity types their questionnaires show.

5 Worksheet 1: Days of the week

1 Circle the days. Then write the days in the diary.

F	R	I	T	A	Y	O	T	T
R	M	O	N	D	A	Y	H	U
I	E	B	T	H	U	R	U	E
D	S	U	N	D	A	Y	R	S
A	S	A	T	U	D	A	S	D
Y	R	T	A	M	O	P	D	A
W	E	D	N	E	S	D	A	Y
S	A	T	U	R	D	A	Y	Y

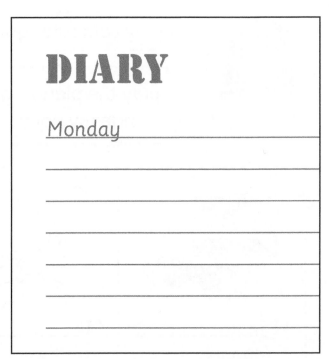

DIARY

Monday

2 Colour the words. Write Thunder and Whisper's favourite days.

My favourite day is
_____ .

My favourite day is
_____ .

Vocabulary: Days of the week

Write. Then cut out the cards and play.

I play computer games on Sundays.

play the piano   go swimming   ~~play computer games~~
ride my pony   ride my bike   play football

1 I _play computer games_ .

4 I _____ _____ .

2 I _____ _____ .

5 I _____ _____ .

3 I _____ _____ .

6 I _____ _____ .

Mondays	Thursdays
Tuesdays	Fridays
Wednesdays	Saturdays

Grammar 1: Present simple, 1st person

© Cambridge University Press 2012 *Super Minds* Teacher's Resource Book Level 1

5 Worksheet 3: Do you ... ?

Ask and answer. Who are you like?

Do you go swimming at the weekend?

Yes, I do.

No, I don't.

swimming / weekend

play football / Mondays

play with your friends / weekend

play in the park / Saturdays

play computer games / Wednesdays

watch TV / Fridays

play with your toys / Tuesdays

play hide and seek / weekend

go to school / Thursdays

ride a bike / Sundays

Grammar 2: *Do you ... ? Yes, I do. / No, I don't.*

5 Worksheet 4: My life

Write your answers to the questions. Then ask your friends.

My favourites	Answer	My friend	My friend	My friend
1 What's your favourite activity at the weekend?				
2 What's your favourite sport?				
3 What's your favourite book?				
4 What's your favourite TV programme?				
5 What's your favourite food?				
6 What's your favourite computer game?				
7 What's your favourite animal?				
8 What's your favourite song?				

Social science: Lifestyle

Super Minds Teacher's Resource Book Level 1   © Cambridge University Press 2012   **PHOTOCOPIABLE**

6 The old house

Worksheet 1: My house

Using the worksheet

- These spelling and observation activities practise vocabulary for rooms in the house *bathroom, bedroom, living room, dining room, hall, kitchen, cellar, stairs, garden* and *What's in the … ?*

- Students complete the word labels for the rooms in the house, then match the questions and answers about the animals hidden in the house.

KEY: Activity 1: **2** bedroom, **3** living room, **4** hall, **5** dining room, **6** stairs, **7** cellar, **8** kitchen, **9** garden; Activity 2: **2**a, **3**c, **4**b

Optional follow-up activity: Students draw their own additional animals on the house picture for their partner to find and answer questions, e.g. *What's in the bathroom? A spider!*

Worksheet 2: There is / There are

Using the worksheet

- This spot the difference activity practises *There's … / There are … .*

- Students look at the two pictures and circle the five differences they find. They can do this individually, then talk about the differences in pairs.

- Students then complete the sentences at the bottom of the worksheet, choosing and circling the correct words.

KEY: Activity 2: **2** there's, a cat; there's, a dog; **3** there are, three; there are, four; **4** there's, a sandwich; there's, a banana; **5** there are, five; there are, four

Optional follow-up activity: Play a memory game with the class. Draw some simple items on the board, e.g. two books, three pencils, a cat, three bananas. Ask students to say what they can see using *There is / are* and then study the board for a couple of minutes. Then ask them to close their eyes while you change some of the details, e.g. add another pencil, add a ruler, rub out two bananas. Students open their eyes again and describe any changes they notice, e.g. *There are four pencils!*

Worksheet 3: How many … ? Is / Are there … ?

Using the worksheet

- This gap-fill activity practises *Is there a … ? Yes, there is. / No, there isn't. Are there any … ? Yes, there are. / No, there aren't* and *How many … are there? There are … .*

- Students look at the pictures and note the differences between them.

- They then read Misty and Thunder's conversations and complete the questions and answers, choosing the correct words from the word banks.

- Students then play the same guessing game in pairs, using the conversations as a model. One student chooses a picture, the other has to guess, using *Is there, Are there* and *How many* questions.

KEY: **2** isn't, **3** there, **4** are, **5** many, **6** are, **7** there, **8** is, **9** How, **10** are, **11** Are, **12** aren't, **13** 2

Optional follow-up activity: Students ask and answer similar questions to find out what their partners have in their pencil case or bag, e.g. *Is there a book? (Yes, there is.) How many books are there? (There are three.)* After asking the questions, students draw or write what they think the contents are, then check by taking the items out of the bag or pencil case.

Worksheet 4: Animal habitats

Using the worksheet

- This card game practises the language needed to talk about different habitats.

- Students cut out their cards. They can play the game in pairs or small groups and with one or more sets of cards. The more cards they use, the harder the game will be.

- Demonstrate the game first with a pair of confident students. Lay out the cards face down in three sets (animals, habitats and habitat features) on the table. Students take turns to choose one card from each set and turn them over. If all three cards match, e.g. *mountains, rocks* and *goat,* they have to make sentences about them and can then keep the set, e.g. *You find rocks on mountains. Goats live in mountains.* If the cards don't match or only two of them match, they must replace them face down on the table and let their partner have a turn.

- The game continues until all the cards are matched up.

Optional follow-up activity: Students find out which habitats exist in different regions of their own country, e.g. Do they have mountains in their country? Do they have jungles? Is their country next to an ocean? Do they have a polar region? They can do this in class, using a world map or globe, or you can ask them to visit the school library or ask their parents. Students can also find out the name of one animal that lives in one of these habitats in their country.

6 Worksheet 1: My house

1 Complete the words.

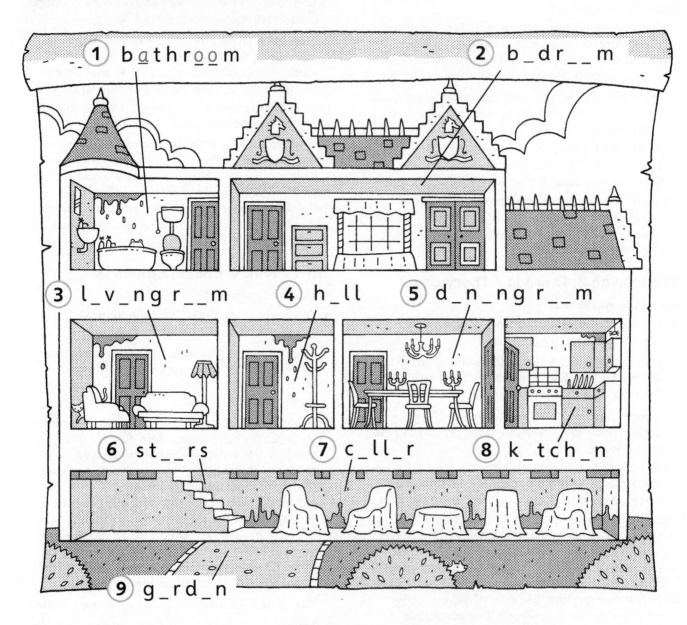

1 b a t h r o o m   2 b _ d r _ _ m

3 l _ v _ n g r _ _ m   4 h _ ll   5 d _ n _ n g r _ _ m

6 st _ _ rs   7 c _ ll _ r   8 k _ tch _ n

9 g _ rd _ n

2 Find the four animals in the picture.
Then read and match.

1 What's in the kitchen?   **a** a frog

2 What's in the bathroom?   **b** a cat

3 What's in the garden?   **c** a dog

4 What's in the living room?   **d** a spider

Vocabulary: The home

1 Circle five differences.

2 Read and circle the correct words.

1 In picture 1, *there's /* (*there are*) *two /* (*three*) *cars.*
   In picture 2, *there's /* (*there are*) (*two*) */ three cars.*

2 In picture 1, *there's / there are a cat / a dog.*
   In picture 2, *there's / there are a cat / a dog.*

3 In picture 1, *there's / there are three / four* books.
   In picture 2, *there's / there are three / four* books.

4 In picture 1, *there's / there are a sandwich / a banana.*
   In picture 2 *there's / there are a sandwich / a banana.*

5 In picture 1, *there's / there are four / five* spiders.
   In picture 2, *there's / there are four / five* spiders.

> Grammar 1: *There is / There are*

© Cambridge University Press 2012   *Super Minds* Teacher's Resource Book Level 1

6 Worksheet 3: How many ... ? Is / Are there ... ?

Write the words, then talk about the pictures.

| ~~Is~~   many   are   are   isn't   there |

[1]___Is___ there a cat?

Are [3]_____ any frogs?

How [5]_____ frogs are there?

It's picture 4!

No, there [2]_____ .

Yes, there [4]_____ .

There [6]_____ three frogs!

| How   are   aren't   there   Are   is |

Is [7]_____ a cat?

[9]_____ many spiders are there?

[11]_____ there any ducks?

It's picture [13]_____ !

Yes, there [8]_____ .

There [10]_____ two spiders!

No, there [12]_____ .

Grammar 2: How many ... ? Is / Are there ...?

Worksheet 4: Animal habitats

Cut out and play.

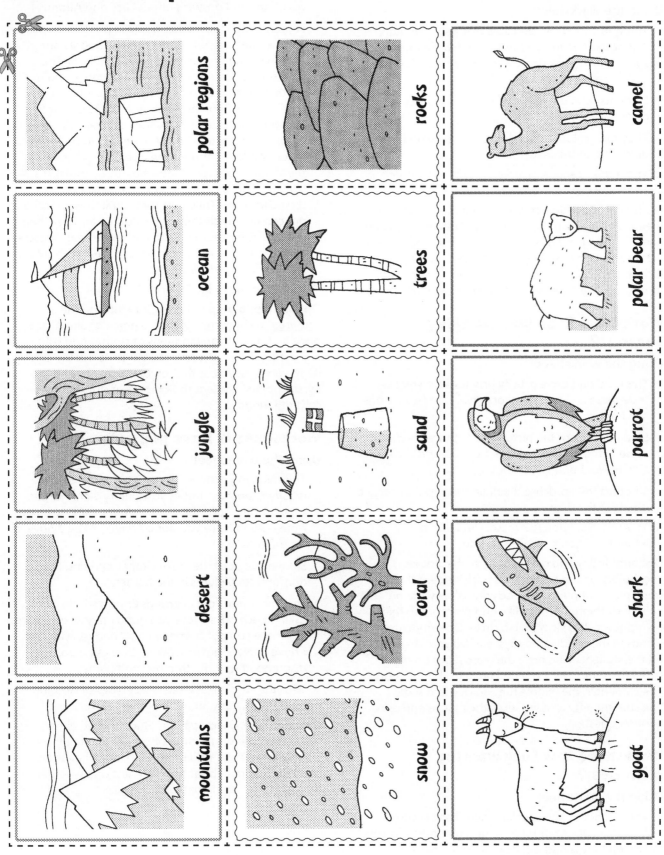

polar regions

rocks

camel

ocean

trees

polar bear

jungle

sand

parrot

desert

coral

shark

mountains

snow

goat

Geography: Habitats

© Cambridge University Press 2012   *Super Minds* Teacher's Resource Book Level 1   39

Worksheet 1: Clothes

Using the worksheet

- This gap-fill activity practises clothes vocabulary *T-shirt, skirt, jeans, trousers, sweater, shoes, cap, socks, shorts, jacket* and *My … is / are …* . It also revises colours.

- Students read the text and write the clothes words after each picture.

- They then colour in the clothes on the washing line, according to the text.

KEY: **2** jeans, **3** shoes, **4** jacket, **5** skirt, **6** trousers, **7** socks, **8** cap, **9** sweater, **10** shorts

Optional follow-up activity: Students write about their own clothes in the same way. Or they can play a guessing game in pairs. They choose another student in the class and describe their clothes as if they are that student, e.g. *My shoes are brown. My skirt is green*, etc. Their partner has to guess who they are.

Worksheet 2: Do you like this / these … ?

Using the worksheet

- This read and circle activity practises *Do you like this / these … ?* and the short answers *Yes, I do* and *No, I don't.*

- Students look at the picture story and write *this* or *these* in the mother's speech bubbles and circle *Yes, I do* or *No, I don't* in the boy's.

- Students then practise the dialogue in pairs and act it out for the class.

KEY: **2** this, No, I don't; **3** these, No, I don't; **4** this, No, I don't; **5** this, Yes, I do.

Optional follow-up activity: Write the clothes vocabulary on the board. Give each student three small pieces of paper. On each one, they write an item of clothing that they like and pin them to their own clothes. The class sit in a circle. One student stands in the middle and says, e.g. *Do you like jeans?* All the students who have the word *jeans* on them stand up, shout *Yes, I do!* and have to change seats. The student in the middle runs quickly to a seat. The student left standing takes their place and asks another question.

Worksheet 3: Is Lucy wearing a sweater?

Using the worksheet

- These reading and speaking activities practise *Is he / she / Lucy wearing a …?* and the short answers *Yes, he / she is* and *No, he / she isn't.* They also revise colours.

- Students look at the pictures and match the questions and answers about Lucy and Adam.

- Students then play a dice game in pairs. Each pair will also need a coin. Each student chooses one of the outline characters (Sheila or Bob) on the worksheet. Student A rolls the dice and, using the 'clothes' dice code, asks a relevant question, e.g. (one spot) *Is Bob / he wearing a cap?* Student B flips the coin. If it's 'heads' they answer, e.g. *Yes, he is*, and if it's 'tails', e.g. *No, he isn't.* If the answer is *Yes*, Student B throws the dice again and, using the 'colour' dice code, says, e.g. (three spots) *It's a yellow cap.* Student A draws and colours this on their character. They take turns until their characters are completely clothed and coloured in. They then describe their characters to each other, e.g. *Sheila's / She's wearing a red T-shirt*, or use them with a new partner for a picture dictation.

KEY: **2**d, **3**a, **4**c/e, **5**f, **6**c/e

Optional follow-up activity: Students use the coloured-in characters to play a game of Bingo (see page 4). Call out combinations of clothes and colours, e.g. *a blue skirt, red jeans*, etc. Students tick the clothes items when they hear the combinations they have used. The first student to tick all their clothes items calls out *Bingo!*

Worksheet 4: Have you got … ?

Using the worksheet

- This mingling activity practises materials *cotton, woollen, leather*, clothes vocabulary *jeans, jacket, socks, shoes, hat, cap, T-shirt, shorts, skirt, sweater, trousers* and *Have you got a / any … ? Yes, I have. / No, I haven't.*

- Students look at the list of clothes and find the appropriate pictures in the border.

- Students then work in groups or as a whole class, asking each other *Have you got a / any …* questions, e.g. *Have you got a woollen hat?* and replying *Yes, I have* or *No, I haven't.* When they get a positive response, they write that person's name.

- With the whole class, see which types of clothing most, hardly any, or none of them have.

Optional follow-up activity: Students find either a real example or a picture of clothes in one of the different materials and bring it to class. They show and tell the class about the materials and whether they are *cool, strong* or *warm* clothes.

7 Worksheet 1: Clothes

Read and write. Then colour the clothes.

| cap sweater shoes ~~T-shirt~~ socks |
| shorts jacket trousers jeans skirt |

My 1 _____T-shirt_____ is pink. My 2 _____ are purple.

My 3 _____ are black. My 4 _____ is green.

My 5 _____ is white. My 6 _____ are brown.

My 7 _____ are red. My 8 _____ is yellow.

My 9 _____ is orange. My 10 _____ are blue.

Vocabulary: Clothes

© Cambridge University Press 2012 *Super Minds* Teacher's Resource Book Level 1

Worksheet 2: Do you like this / these ... ?

Write *this* or *these*. Then circle the answers.

Grammar 1: *Do you like this / these ...? Yes, I do. No, I don't.*

7 # Worksheet 3: Is Lucy wearing a sweater?

1 ## Match the questions and answers.

Adam

1 Is Lucy wearing a sweater?
2 Is Adam wearing a cap?
3 Is Lucy wearing shoes?
4 Is Adam wearing socks?
5 Is Lucy wearing jeans?
6 Is Adam wearing a T-shirt?

a Yes, she is.
b No, she isn't.
c No, he isn't.
d Yes, he is.
e No, he isn't.
f No, she isn't.

Lucy

2 ## Throw the dice to dress and colour Bob and Sheila.

Is Bob wearing a cap?

Yes, he is. It's a yellow cap!

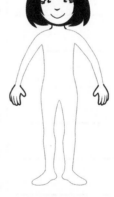

Sheila

Bob

Clothes

Colours

 blue

 red

 yellow

 green

 orange

 brown

> Grammar 2: Present continuous, 3rd person

 © Cambridge University Press 2012 *Super Minds* Teacher's Resource Book Level 1

Worksheet 4: Have you got ... ?

Ask questions and write the names of students in your class.

Have you got ... ?

_____ has got cotton shoes.

_____ has got a woollen jacket.

_____ has got a woollen hat.

_____ has got a cotton T-shirt.

_____ has got cotton jeans.

_____ has got woollen socks.

_____ has got a leather cap.

_____ has got cotton shorts.

_____ has got a woollen sweater.

_____ has got a leather jacket.

_____ has got a cotton skirt.

_____ has got cotton trousers.

Science: Materials

Super Minds Teacher's Resource Book Level 1   © Cambridge University Press 2012   **PHOTOCOPIABLE**

8 The robot

Worksheet 1: The body

Using the worksheet

- This anagram activity practises vocabulary for parts of the body *head, hand, arm, fingers, knee, leg, foot, toes* and numbers up to 16.

- Students solve the anagrams and draw lines from the words to the relevant part of the robot.

- Students then fill in the robot's sentences with either numbers or words.

KEY: Activity 1: **2** hand, **3** knee, **4** toes, **5** arm, **6** fingers, **7** leg, **8** foot; Activity 2: **2** four, **3** sixteen, **4** six, **5** twelve, **6** three

Optional follow-up activity: Play a game of *How many … ?* Ask six volunteers in the class to stand up. Call out combinations of numbers and body parts, e.g. *four heads, three arms, fifteen fingers*. Students arrange themselves in different combinations to show that number of body parts, e.g. lean four of their heads together, hold up 15 fingers between them, etc.

Worksheet 2: I can …

Using the worksheet

- This writing activity practises *I can / I can't … .*

- Students look at the chart to see what the characters can and can't do. They complete the speech bubbles, choosing *can* or *can't* each time.

- Students then use the worksheet to play a guessing or memory game in pairs. One student reads out one of the speech bubbles while the other listens without looking at the worksheet. He or she guesses which character they are from the description of what they can and can't do, e.g. *I can skip. I can touch my toes. I can't stand on one leg. (You're Flash!)*

KEY: Misty *can / can / can*; Thunder *can / can't / can*; Flash *can / can / can't*; Whisper *can't / can / can*

Optional follow-up activity: Make up instructions for students to try, e.g. *Touch your knees with your nose, Stand on your hands*, etc., and see which ones students can achieve! Encourage students to say, e.g. *I can / can't touch my knees with my nose*, accordingly. Students can also report on what other children in the class can do, e.g. *Anna can stand on her hands!*

Worksheet 3: Can you … ?

Using the worksheet

- This board game practises actions *ride a horse / bike, dance, play football / tennis / the piano, swim, skip*, question form *Can you … ?* and short answers *Yes, I can / No, I can't*. Students will need counters and a coin to play the game.

- Students play in pairs. They each choose a robot they want to be and look at the chart to see what they can and can't do. They put their counters at the start of the game.

- Student A throws a coin. If it's 'heads', they move forward one square. If it's 'tails' they move forward two squares. Student B asks the appropriate *Can you … ?* question for the activity in the square that A has landed on, e.g. *Can you swim?* Student A checks the robot chart for their own chosen robot and answers *Yes, I can*, or *No, I can't* accordingly. If they answer *Yes, I can*, they stay where they are. If they answer *No, I can't*, they move back one space.

- The winner is the first robot to reach the finishing line.

Optional follow-up activity: Play a messages game. Students write one *Can you … ?* question on a slip of paper, e.g. *Can you ride a horse?* Fold these up and put them into a bag. Students take turns to choose a question and read it out loud. They nominate another student to answer and demonstrate the activity if they say they can do it.

Worksheet 4: Animal skeletons

Using the worksheet

- This craft and reading activity practises animal vocabulary *owl, crocodile, rat* and *frog*. It also revises using *can* and *can't* with actions.

- Students make animal X-ray pictures by cutting out the animal outlines at the bottom of the worksheet and sticking them over the correct animal skeletons. (Tell students to glue only the borders of the pictures.) When the pictures are stuck together, ask students to hold them up to the light. They will see the skeletons appear as if by magic!

- Students circle the correct words on the fact cards to complete the description of each animal.

KEY: **1** *big / can / can / can't*, **2** *small / can't / can't / can*, **3** *small / can / can / can't*, **4** *small / can / can / can't*

Optional follow-up activity: Students play a game of *Twenty Questions*, using questions with *Is it … ?* or *Can it … ?* (*Is it green? Can it fly?* etc.) One student thinks of an animal and the others have to guess what it is by asking a maximum of 20 *Yes/No* questions.

1 Write the words. Then match.

| fingers | toes | ~~head~~ | foot | knee | arm | hand | leg |

1 deah ___head___

2 nahd _____

3 neek _____

4 sote _____

5 ram _____

6 grensif _____

7 elg _____

8 tofo _____

2 How many? Count and write.

1 I've got ___one___ head.
2 I've got _____ arms.
3 I've got _____ fingers.

4 I've got _____ knees.
5 I've got _____ toes.
6 I've got _____ legs.

Vocabulary: The body

Write *can* or *can't*. Then play a guessing game.

🤸 skip	✓	✓	✓	✗
🤸 touch toes	✓	✗	✓	✓
🤸 stand on one leg	✓	✓	✗	✓

Misty: I ___*can*___ skip.
I _____ touch my toes.
I _____ stand on one leg.

Thunder: I _____ skip.
I _____ touch my toes.
I _____ stand on one leg.

Flash: I _____ skip.
I _____ touch my toes.
I _____ stand on one leg.

Whisper: I _____ skip.
I _____ touch my toes.
I _____ stand on one leg.

(Grammar 1: *can / can't* for ability)

© Cambridge University Press 2012 *Super Minds* Teacher's Resource Book Level 1

⑧ Worksheet 3: Can you ... ?

Play the robot race.

	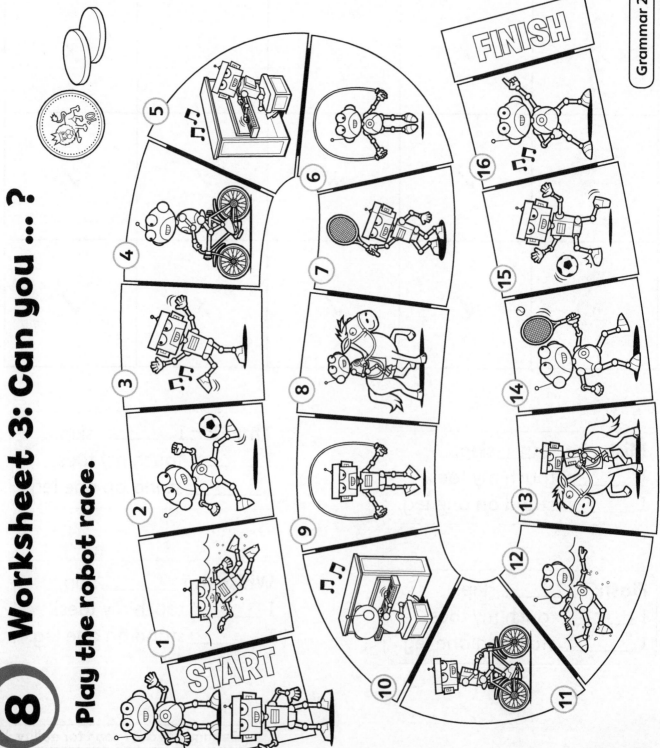 🤖	🐸
ride a horse	x	✓
swim	✓	x
play football	x	✓
dance	✓	x
ride a bike	✓	x
play the piano	x	✓
skip	x	x
play tennis	✓	✓

START

FINISH

1 2 3 4 5 6 7 8 9 10 11 12 13 14 15 16

Grammar 2: Questions with *can* for ability

Super Minds Teacher's Resource Book Level 1   © Cambridge University Press 2012   **PHOTOCOPIABLE**

8 Worksheet 4: Animal skeletons

Cut and stick. Then read and choose.

1 Crocodile

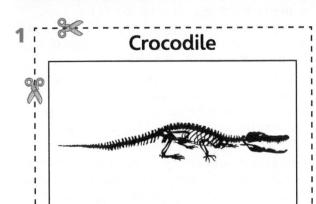

This animal is (big) / small. It is green and brown. It can / can't swim and it can / can't walk. It can / can't fly.

2 Owl

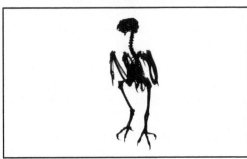

This animal is big / small and brown. It can / can't climb and it can / can't swim. It can / can't fly.

3 Rat

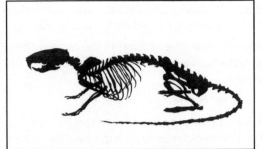

This animal is big / small and brown. It can / can't swim and it can / can't run. It can / can't fly.

4 Frog

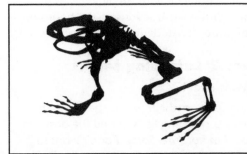

This animal is big / small. It's green and brown. It can / can't jump and it can / can't swim. It can / can't run.

a
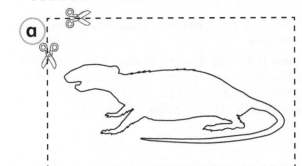

b

c
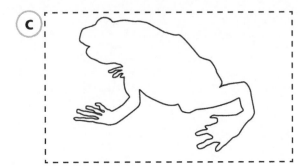

d
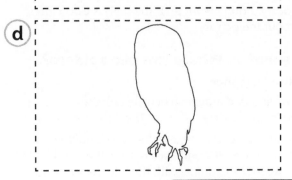

⑨ At the beach

Worksheet 1: Catch a fish!

Using the worksheet

- This reading and writing activity practises the vocabulary for holidays *catch a fish, look for shells, paint a picture, read a book, take a photo, eat ice cream, listen to music, make a sandcastle.*

- Students can do this as a memory game from the picture on Student's Book page 106. They draw the missing details in the pictures in pencil and complete the captions using the word bank, before checking.

KEY: 2 look, **3** paint, **4** read, **5** take, **6** make, **7** eat, **8** listen

Optional follow-up activity: Play a game of *Simon says!* (see page 4), using these new actions and other actions that students know in English. When you say *Simon says*, e.g. *Simon says make a sandcastle*, they have to mime the action. If you give any instructions without *Simon says*, e.g. *Make a sandcastle*, students do nothing. Alternatively, you can play this as a reading game, writing instructions on the board or small slips of paper for students to read and act out.

Worksheet 2: Let's play tennis.

Using the worksheet

- This writing and matching activity practises the language of suggesting *Let's ...* and the answers *Good idea, I'm not sure, Sorry, I don't want to.* It also practises vocabulary for holiday activities.

- Students complete the suggestion in each speech bubble, using the words in the word bank, then read the answer and circle the correct matching picture.

KEY: 2 picture, b; **3** TV, b; **4** sandcastle, a; **5** music, a; **6** book, b

Optional follow-up activity: Students play a suggestions game in class. Each student writes a suggestion on a piece of paper, e.g. *Let's ride a horse.* They fold these up and put them into a box or bag. Students then take it in turns to take a piece of paper and read out the suggestion to another student in the class. That student replies with *Good idea, I'm not sure* or *Sorry, I don't want to.* If the reply is *Good idea*, they act out the activity.

Worksheet 3: Where are the spiders?

Using the worksheet

- This writing and matching activity practises *Where's / Where are ...? , It's / They're in the ... .*

- Students read and complete the speech bubbles choosing *'s, are, It's* and *They're* from the word bank. Read the example with them to demonstrate.

- Students then read the dialogues again and connect the pictures at the bottom of the worksheet correctly. They say where the objects are as they do so, e.g. *The spiders are in the pencil case. The pencil case is in the classroom.*

KEY: Activity 1: a are, **b** They're, **c** 's, **d** It's. This sequence is repeated in each dialogue; **Activity 2:** Students should draw connecting lines between: **2** sandwiches, bag, kitchen; **3** frogs, toy box, bedroom; **4** apples, tree, garden

Optional follow-up activity: Students play a memory game using the worksheet. In pairs, one student looks at the worksheet and asks questions, e.g. *Where's the pencil case?* The other student has to answer from memory. Students can also hide their own things somewhere in the classroom and ask and answer questions to find them.

Worksheet 4: It's hot.

Using the worksheet

- This craft activity practises weather vocabulary *It's hot, sunny, cold, snowing, raining, cloudy.*

- Students label the pictures in the circle with the correct weather words. They then colour in the pictures.

- They then cut the two shapes out.

- Students make the weather wheel by attaching the 'The weather today' shape over the circle with a butterfly clip. When they turn the top shape, the different weather types will appear one by one.

- Students can keep this weather wheel to show the different weather types for each day and say what they are.

KEY: 2 sunny, **3** cold/cloudy, **4** cloudy/cold, **5** raining, **6** snowing

Optional follow-up activity: Students decide which is their favourite weather type, e.g. *I like sunny weather.* They then conduct a class survey to find out which weather type is the most popular in the class.

9 Worksheet 1: Catch a fish!

Look and draw. Then write.

paint ~~catch~~ make look read eat listen take

1 _catch_ a fish

2 _____ for shells

3 _____ a picture

4 _____ a book

5 _____ a photo

6 _____ a sandcastle

7 _____ ice cream

8 _____ to music

Vocabulary: Holidays

© Cambridge University Press 2012 *Super Minds* Teacher's Resource Book Level 1

Worksheet 2: Let's play tennis.

Write. Then read, match and circle.

sandcastle   music   ~~tennis~~   picture   book   TV

1 Let's play __tennis__ .   **a**   **b**

Good idea.

2 Let's paint a _____ .   **a**   **b**

Sorry, I don't want to.

3 Let's watch _____ .   **a**   **b**

I'm not sure.

4 Let's make a _____ .   **a**   **b**

Good idea.

5 Let's listen to _____ .   **a**   **b**

Sorry, I don't want to.

6 Let's read a _____ .   **a**   **b**

I'm not sure.

Grammar 1: Suggestions

Super Minds Teacher's Resource Book Level 1   © Cambridge University Press 2012   **PHOTOCOPIABLE**

9 Worksheet 3: Where are the spiders?

1 Read and complete.

They're   's   are   It's

1 Where ª _____are_____ the spiders?
Where ᶜ _____'s_____ the pencil case?

ᵇ _They're_ in the pencil case.
ᵈ _It's_ in the classroom.

2 Where ª _____ the sandwiches?
Where ᶜ _____ the bag?

ᵇ _____ in the bag.
ᵈ _____ in the kitchen.

3 Where ª _____ the frogs?
Where ᶜ _____ the toy box?

ᵇ _____ in the toy box.
ᵈ _____ in the bedroom.

4 Where ª _____ the apples?
Where ᶜ _____ the tree?

ᵇ _____ on the tree.
ᵈ _____ in the garden.

2 Now read again and match.

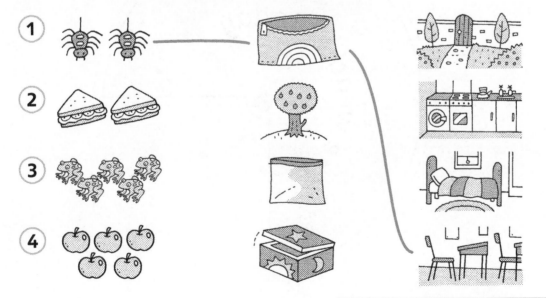

Grammar 2: *Where is / Where are … ?*

Worksheet 4: It's hot.

Write and colour. Then make a weather wheel.

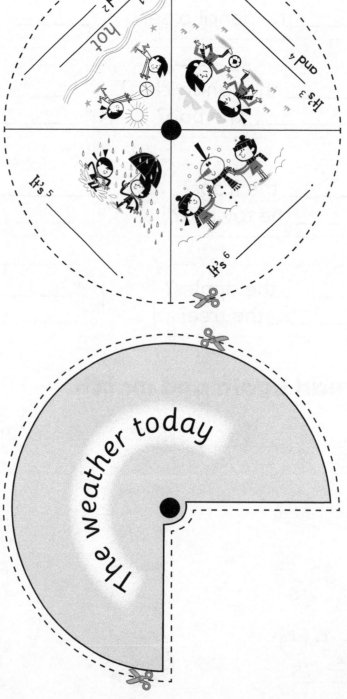

sunny   snowing   raining   cloudy   cold   ~~hot~~

Geography: Holiday weather

Progress test 1: Listening

Name _____

D 2 Listen and circle.

1. a  b

2. a  b

3. a  b

4. a  b

5. a  b

6. a  b

Progress test 2: Reading

Name _____

Read, find and colour.

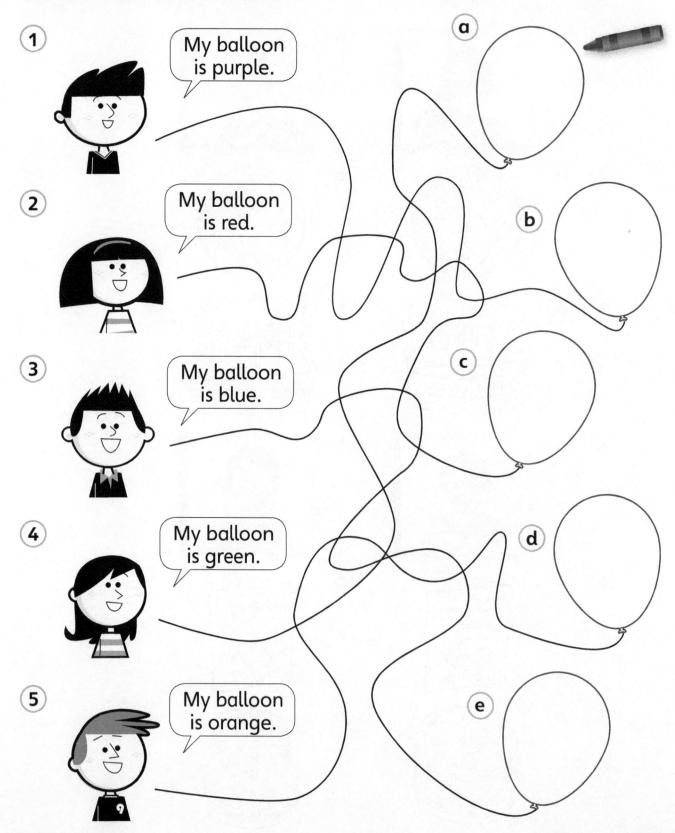

1. My balloon is purple.
2. My balloon is red.
3. My balloon is blue.
4. My balloon is green.
5. My balloon is orange.

a
b
c
d
e

Super Minds Teacher's Resource Book Level 1   © Cambridge University Press 2012

Name _____

Match the questions and answers. Draw lines.

1 What's this?

a It's a chair.

2 Is it a book?

b It's a book.

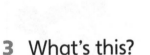

3 What's this?

c Yes, it is.

4 What's this?

d It's a pencil.

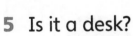

5 Is it a desk?

e No, it isn't.

6 What's this?

f It's a ruler.

© Cambridge University Press 2012   *Super Minds* Teacher's Resource Book Level 1

Progress test 2: Listening

Name _____

CD 3 **Listen and number.**

a

1

b

c

d

e

f

Super Minds Teacher's Resource Book Level 1 © Cambridge University Press 2012 **PHOTOCOPIABLE**

Name _____

Choose and circle the words.

1

(His) / Her name's Fred.
He's / She's eight.
The ball is his
favourite toy.

2

His / Her name's
Olivia.
He's / She's six.
Her favourite toy
is a doll.

3

His name's Joe.
He's / She's seven.
His favourite toy is
his bike / go-kart.

Name _____

 Listen and circle the pictures.

1 **a** 　　**b**

2 **a** 　　**b**

3 **a** 　　**b**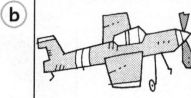

4 **a** 　　**b**

5 **a** 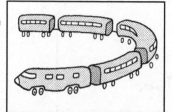　　**b**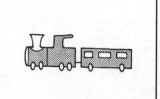

6 **a** 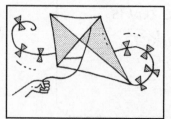　　**b**

Name _____

 Listen and circle.

1 (a)  (b)

2 (a)  (b)

3 (a)  (b)

4 (a)  (b)

5 (a)  (b)

6 (a)  (b)

3 Progress test 2: Reading

Name _____

Read and match.

1.    **a** I like spiders.

2.    **b** I like dogs.

3.    **c** ~~I don't like dogs.~~

4.    **d** I don't like spiders.

5.    **e** I like cats, too.

6.    **f** I don't like cats.

Name _____

Read and write ✓ or ✗.

> I've got ~~apples~~ and I've got bananas.
> I haven't got carrots. I've got cake.
> I haven't got pizza. I've got cheese.

I've got …

✓

Name _____

CD 6 **Listen, look and circle the correct answer.**

1 Yes, we have. / (No, we haven't.)

2 Yes, we have. / No, we haven't.

3 Yes, we have. / No, we haven't.

4 Yes, we have. / No, we haven't.

5 Yes, we have. / No, we haven't.

6 Yes, we have. / No, we haven't.

Name _____

Listen and tick (✓).

Ben's week

Monday						
Tuesday						
Wednesday						
Thursday				✓		
Friday						
Saturday						

Name _____

Read and complete.

Do   don't   play   do   watch   go

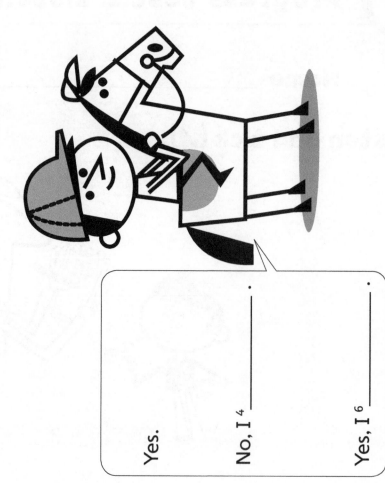

1 _Do_ ___ you
2 _____ swimming on
Saturdays?

Do you
3 _____ TV
at the weekend?

Do you
5 _____ computer games
on Sundays?

Yes.

No, I 4 _____ .

Yes, I 6 _____ .

Super Minds Teacher's Resource Book Level 1   © Cambridge University Press 2012   **PHOTOCOPIABLE**

Name _____

Listen and draw lines.

6 Progress test 2: Reading

Name _____

1 **Read and tick (✓) picture 1 or picture 2.**

Picture 1   Picture 2

1   There are two cats in the tree.   picture 1 ✓   picture 2 ☐

2   There's a lizard on the go-kart.   picture 1 ☐   picture 2 ☐

3   There are two frogs in the garden.   picture 1 ☐   picture 2 ☐

2 **Match the questions and answers.**

1   Is there a cat in picture 2?   **a**   There are two.

2   Is there a lizard in picture 1?   **b**   Yes, there are.

3   Are there any spiders in picture 2?   **c**   Yes, there is.

4   How many ducks are there in picture 1?   **d**   No, there isn't.

Super Minds Teacher's Resource Book Level 1   © Cambridge University Press 2012   **PHOTOCOPIABLE**

Name _____

Listen and write ✓ or X.

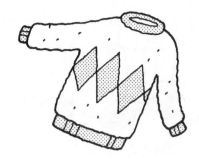 ☐

 ☐

 ☐

 ☐

 ☐

© Cambridge University Press 2012   *Super Minds* Teacher's Resource Book Level 1

Name _____

Read and colour.

Amy

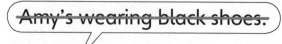

~~Amy's wearing black shoes.~~

Is she wearing a pink T-shirt?

Yes, she is.

Is she wearing a red skirt?

No, she isn't. She's wearing a purple skirt.

Harry

Harry isn't wearing a brown sweater. His sweater's green.

Is he wearing blue jeans?

Yes, he is.

Is he wearing yellow socks?

No, he isn't. They're orange.

Super Minds Teacher's Resource Book Level 1   © Cambridge University Press 2012

Name _____

Read and match.

1 I can't sing. | f |
2 I can skip on one leg. | |
3 I can touch my knees. | |
4 I can't stand on my hands. | |
5 I can't touch my toes. | |
6 I can stand on one leg. | |

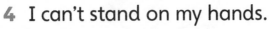

© Cambridge University Press 2012 *Super Minds* Teacher's Resource Book Level 1

Name _____

CD 10 **Listen and write numbers next to the pictures.**

a

b  `1`

c  ☐

d  ☐

e  ☐

f  ☐

g  ☐

h  ☐

i  ☐

Super Minds Teacher's Resource Book Level 1   © Cambridge University Press 2012   **PHOTOCOPIABLE**

Name _____

Complete. Then match.

sure ~~make~~ eat want listen idea

1. Let's ᵃ__make__ a sandcastle.

   Good ᵇ_____ !

2. Let's ᵃ_____ ice cream.

   Sorry, I don't ᵇ_____ to.

3. Let's ᵃ_____ to music.

   I'm not ᵇ_____ .

Name _____

CD 11 **Listen and look. Circle the correct answer.**

1   a   (It's under the chair.)   b   They're under the chair.

2   a   It's on the sandcastle.   b   They're on the sandcastle.

3   a   It's on the beach.   b   They're on the beach.

4   a   It's in the sea.   b   They're in the sea.

5   a   It's on the sandcastle.   b   They're on the sandcastle.

6   a   It's in the bag.   b   They're in the bag.

Progress tests

Introduction to the progress tests

There are two progress tests for each of the ten units in the Level 1 Student's Book: a listening test and a reading or reading and writing test. These activities cover the unit vocabulary and grammar seen on the first, second and fourth pages of each unit in the Student's Book and Workbook.

There are five questions in each progress test and an example. Each test is marked out of 5 so that the total mark for both progress tests in the unit is 10. Each test should take 10 to 20 minutes of class time.

The progress tests can be used in a number of ways. You might choose to do them both together at the end of a unit. Or you might choose to do one of the two progress tests once students have completed the first half of each unit of the Student's Book and Workbook and then save the other test until students have completed the entire unit. Alternatively, you might choose to do one of the two tests at the end of each unit and then save the other test until the end of term. This staged approach will help you to see what students have learnt and understood in the short term and what they can remember in the long term. It will also give students an opportunity to revise / ask for help between tests in order to improve their mark.

Friends
Progress test 1: Listening

Listen and circle.

Students listen and circle the correct picture in questions 2 to 6.

TAPESCRIPT

1
Interviewer: Hello. What's your name?
Misty: I'm Misty.

2
Interviewer: And how old are you, Misty?
Misty: I'm six.

3
Interviewer: How old are you, Flash?
Flash: I'm eight.

4
Interviewer: And what's your name?
Thunder: I'm Thunder!

5
Interviewer: And how old are you, Thunder?
Thunder: I'm seven.

6
Interviewer: What about you, Whisper? How old are you?
Whisper: I'm eight.

KEY: 2a (6), **3**b (eight candles), **4**a (Thunder), **5**b (7), **6**b (8)

Friends
Progress test 2: Reading

Read, find and colour.

Students follow the tangled lines and colour in the balloons correctly. They will need access to purple, blue, red, green and orange crayons or coloured pencils.

KEY: 1b (the balloon should be coloured purple), **2**c (the balloon should be coloured red), **3**e (the balloon should be coloured blue), **4**a (the balloon should be coloured green), **5**d (the balloon should be coloured orange)

Unit 1
Progress test 1: Reading

Match the questions and answers.
Draw lines.

Students read the questions and match them to the correct answers by drawing lines.

KEY: 2e, **3**f, **4**a, **5**c, **6**b

Unit 1
Progress test 2: Listening

Listen and number.

Students listen and number the pictures 2 to 6.

TAPESCRIPT
1 Sit at your desk.
2 Open your pencil case, please.
3 Pass me a ruler, please.
4 Pass me a pencil, please.
5 Close your book.
6 Pass me a rubber, please.

KEY: b2, **c6**, **d4**, **e3**, **f5**

Unit 2
Progress test 1: Reading

Choose and circle the words.

Students read and circle the correct words in the sentences.

KEY: 1 He's; **2** Her, She's; **3** He's, go-kart

Unit 2

Progress test 2: Listening

Listen and circle the pictures.

Students listen and circle the correct picture in each pair.

TAPESCRIPT
1 It's a small car.
2 It's a beautiful doll.
3 It's an old plane.
4 It's an ugly monster.
5 It's a long train.
6 It's a big kite.

KEY: 2a, 3b, 4b, 5a, 6a

Unit 3

Progress test 1: Listening

Listen and circle.

Students listen and circle the correct picture in each pair.

TAPESCRIPT
1 The dog is under the desk.
2 The spider is in the pencil case.
3 The monster is under the chair.
4 The rat is in the bag.
5 The duck is under the plane.
6 The elephant is on the chair.

KEY: 2a, 3b, 4b, 5b, 6a

Unit 3

Progress test 2: Reading

Read and match.

Students read the sentences and match them to the pictures.

KEY: 2b, 3e, 4f, 5a, 6d

Unit 4

Progress test 1: Reading

Read and write ✓ or ✗.

Students read the speech bubble. They write a tick on the list next to the foods the mother has got and a cross next to the foods she hasn't got.

KEY: cheese ✓, cake ✓, bananas ✓, carrots ✗, pizza ✗

Unit 4

Progress test 2: Listening

Listen, look and circle the correct answer.

Students listen to the questions, look at the picture and circle the correct answer each time.

TAPESCRIPT
1
Girl: Dad, have we got any sandwiches?
2
Girl: Aw!!! Have we got any chicken?
3
Boy: And Dad. Have we got any sausages?
4
Girl: What about steak? Have we got any steak?
5
Boy: And carrots. Have we got any carrots?
6
Both children: Have we got any cake?

KEY: 2 Yes, we have. 3 Yes, we have. 4 No, we haven't. 5 Yes, we have. 6 No, we haven't.

Unit 5

Progress test 1: Listening

Listen and tick (✓).

Students listen and tick the day that Ben does each activity.

TAPESCRIPT
1
Interviewer: Hello, Ben. Tell me about your week. Do you go swimming?
Ben: Yes. I go swimming on Thursdays.
2
Interviewer: And what about football?
Ben: I play football on Mondays.
Interviewer: OK.
3
Ben: And I've got a pony. I ride my pony on Tuesdays.
4
Interviewer: And what about the weekend?
Ben: Well, I ride my bike. I ride my bike on Saturdays.
5
Interviewer: Do you play computer games at the weekend, too?
Ben: No. I play computer games on Fridays.
6
Interviewer: And TV?
Ben: Oh, yes. I watch football on TV on Wednesdays.

KEY: Monday, play football; Tuesday, ride my pony; Wednesday, watch TV; Friday, play computer games; Saturday, ride my bike

Unit 5

Progress test 2: Reading and writing

Read and complete.

Students complete the conversation between the two boys with words from the word box.

KEY: 2 go, **3** watch, **4** don't, **5** play, **6** do

Unit 6
Progress test 1: Listening

Listen and draw lines.

Students listen and draw lines to match the animals or objects to the correct room.

TAPESCRIPT
1 There's a spider in the cellar.
2 There's a dog in the dining room.
3 There's a cat in the living room.
4 There's a doll in the bedroom.
5 There's a book in the kitchen.
6 There's a bike in the hall.

KEY: Students should match the animals or objects and rooms as follows:
2 dog / dining room, **3** cat / living room, **4** doll / bedroom, **5** book / kitchen, **6** bike / hall

Unit 6
Progress test 2: Reading

 Read and tick (✓) picture 1 or picture 2.

Students read the sentences and decide if they apply to picture **1** or picture **2**. They then write a tick in the correct box.

KEY: 2 picture 2; **3** picture 2

 Match the questions and answers.

Students read the sentences and find the correct answers, referring to pictures 1 and 2 again.

KEY: 2d, **3**b, **4**a

Unit 7
Progress test 1: Listening

Listen and write ✓ or ✗.

Students listen to the dialogue and write ticks or crosses next to the clothes, according to whether Harry likes them or not.

TAPESCRIPT
1
Mother: Harry. Do you like these trousers?
Harry: Er ... no, I don't. Sorry.
2
Mother: Do you like these jeans?
Harry: Yes, I do. They're really nice.
3
Mother: What about this sweater? Do you like this sweater?
Harry: No, I don't.
4
Mother: Hmm. Do you like this cap?

Harry: Yes, I do.
5
Mother: What about this T-shirt? Do you like this T-shirt?
Harry: Yes, I do.
6
Mother: And do you like these shoes?
Harry: No, I don't. They're horrible!

KEY: Students should tick the jeans, cap and T-shirt. They should draw a cross next to the sweater and shoes.

Unit 7
Progress test 2: Reading

Read and colour.

Students read the speech bubbles and colour Amy and Harry's clothes correctly. They will need blue, green, pink, purple and orange crayons.

KEY: Clothes should be coloured as follows: Amy: pink T-shirt, purple skirt; Harry: green sweater, blue jeans, orange socks

Unit 8
Progress test 1: Reading

Read and match.

Students read the sentences and write the letter of the picture that matches.

KEY: 2c, **3**g, **4**e, **5**b, **6**d

Unit 8
Progress test 2: Listening

Listen and write numbers next to the pictures.

Students listen to the dialogues and write the number of the dialogue next to the appropriate picture.
NB Not all of the pictures are mentioned in the dialogues. There are three which will have no number next to them.

TAPESCRIPT
1
Interviewer: Sally. What can you do? Can you skip?
Girl: Yes, I can.
2
Interviewer: Can you play tennis?
Girl: No, I can't.
3
Interviewer: Can you swim?
Boy: No, I can't.
4
Interviewer: Can you ride a horse?
Boy: Yes, I can! That's easy!

5

Interviewer: And can you dance?

Girl: Yes, I can.

6

Interviewer: What can you do? Can you play the piano?

Boy: Er. No, I can't.

KEY: 2e, 3i, 4g, 5c, 6h

Unit 9

Progress test 1: Reading and writing

Complete. Then match.

Students read and complete the speech bubbles with the correct words from the word box.

KEY: 1b idea, 2a eat, 2b want, 3a listen, 3b sure

Unit 9

Progress test 2: Listening

Listen and look. Circle the correct answer.

Students listen to the questions and look at the picture. They choose and circle the correct answer each time.

TAPESCRIPT
1 Where's the ball?
2 Where are the shells?
3 Where's the bag?
4 Where are the fish?
5 Where are the birds?
6 Where's the book?

KEY: 2b, 3a, 4b, 5b, 6a